VOLUME 2

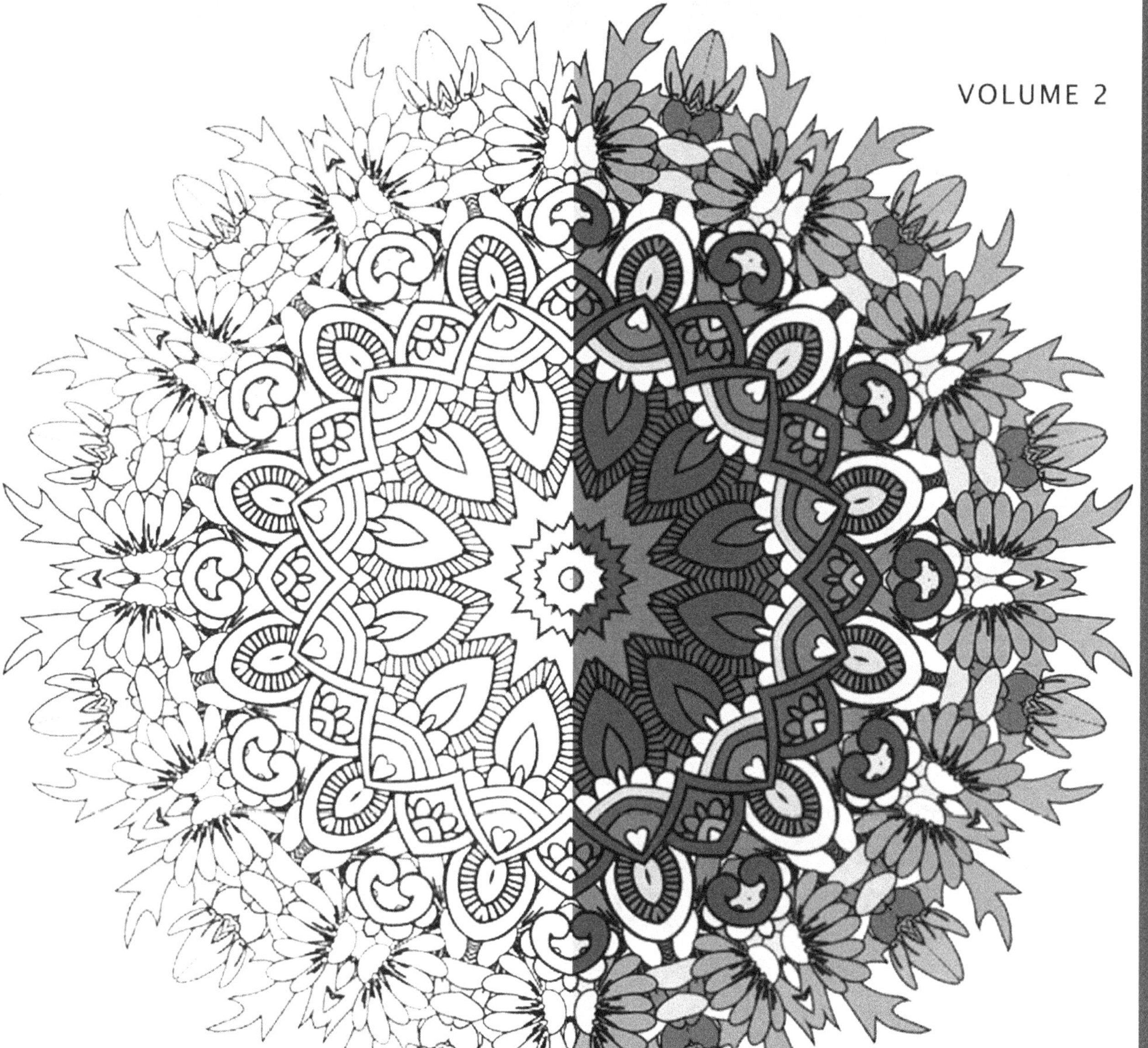

FLOWER
MANDALAS

COLORING BOOK FOR ADULTS

COLOR TEST PAGE

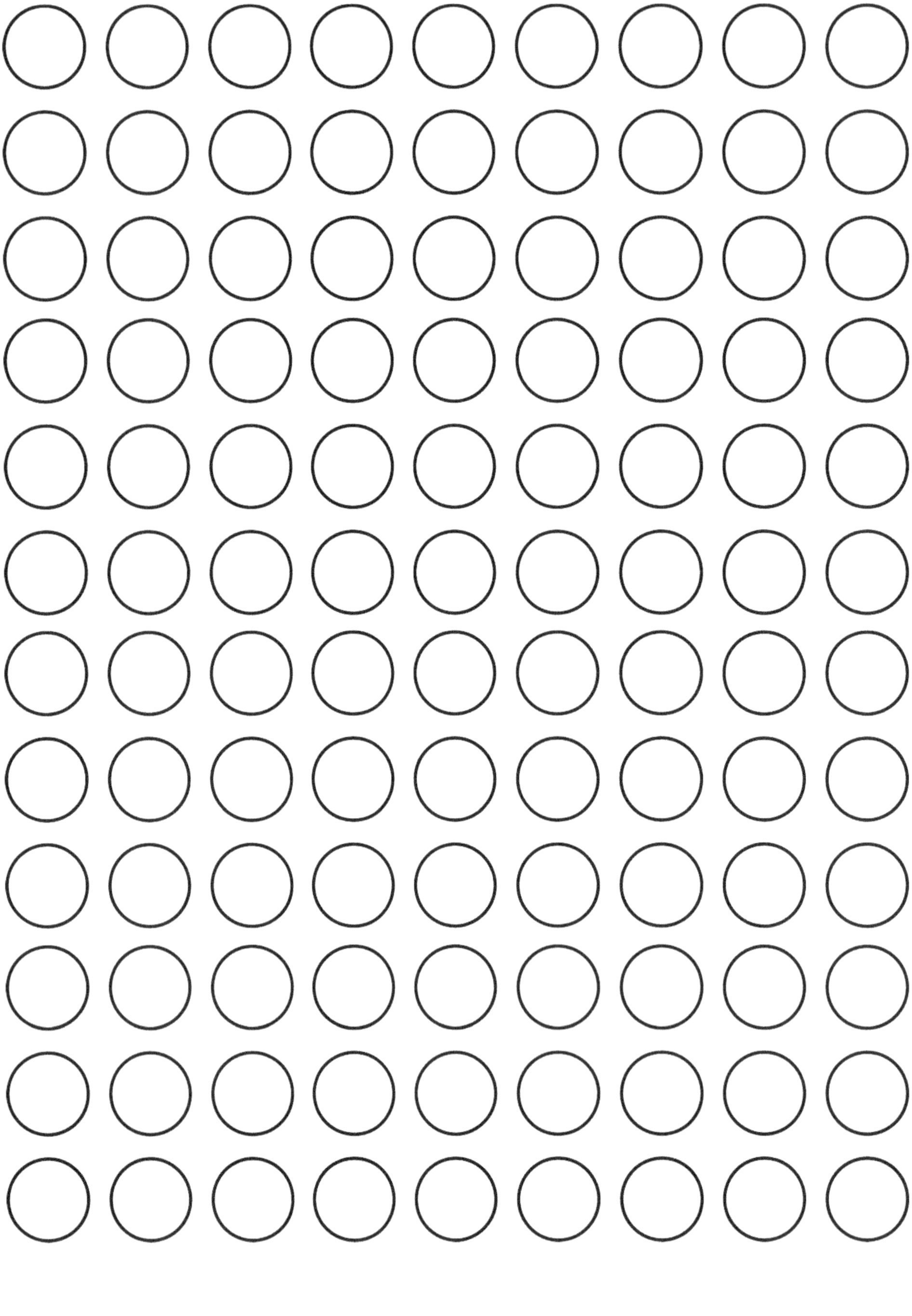

COLOR TEST PAGE

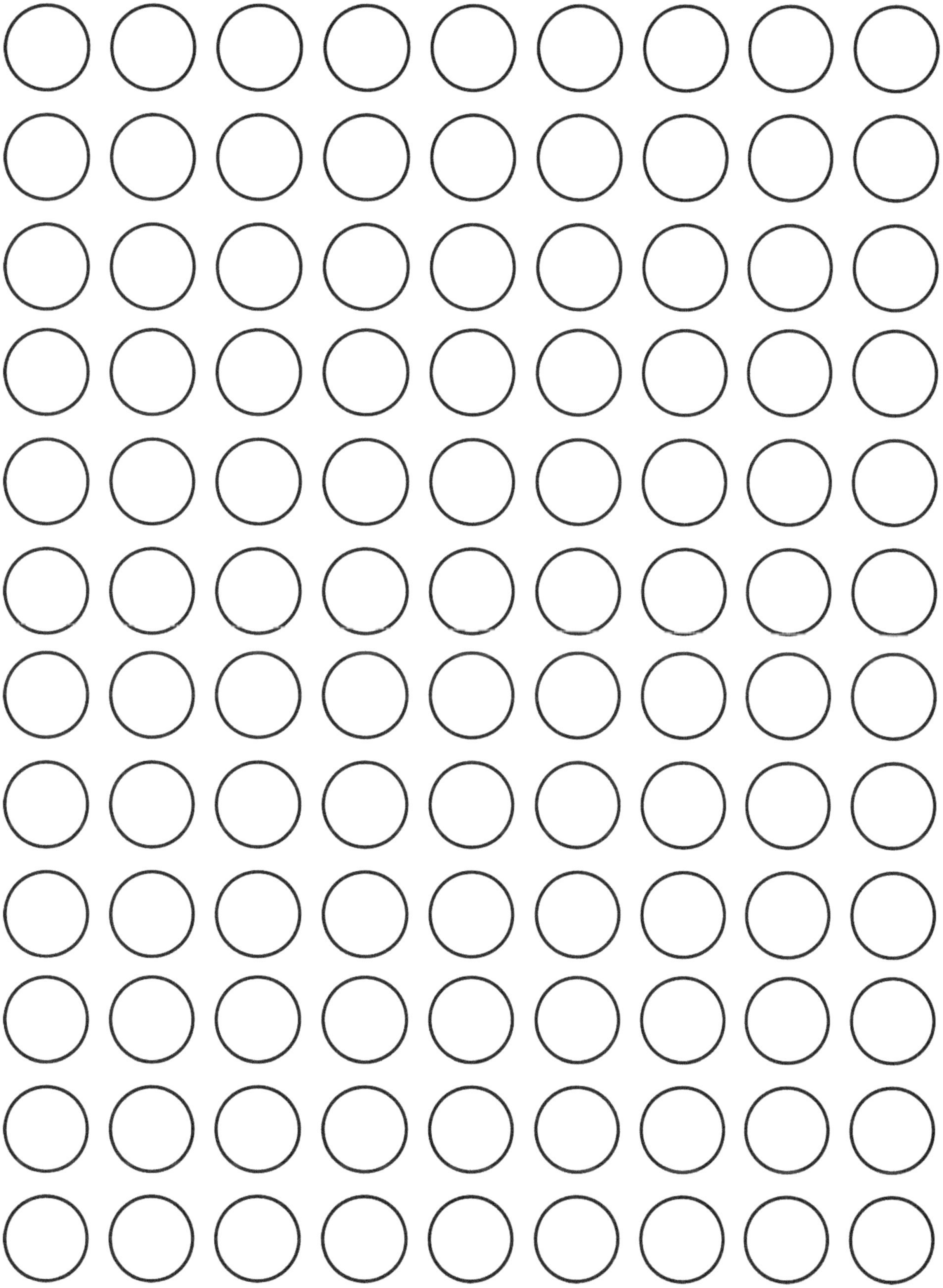

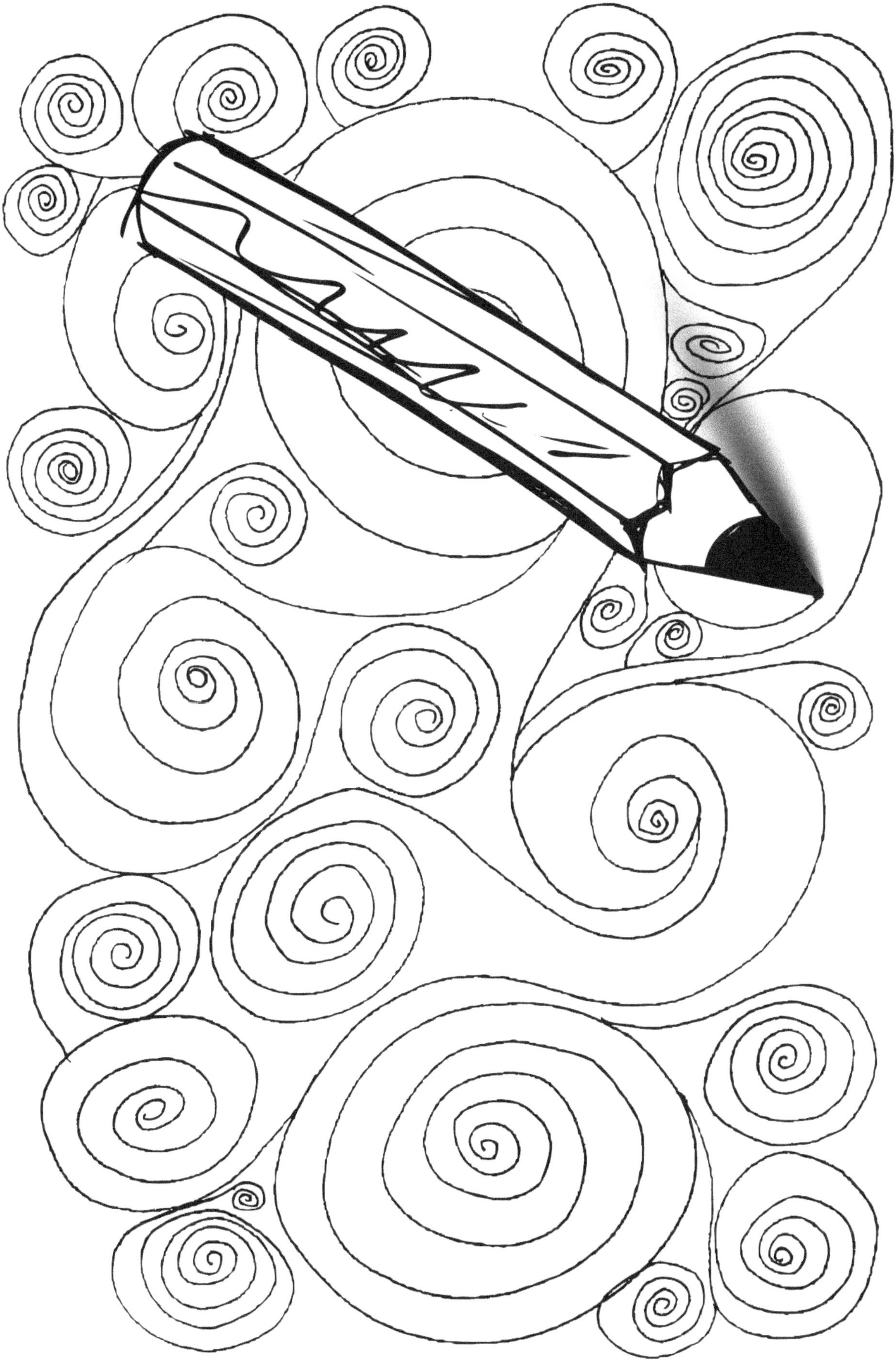

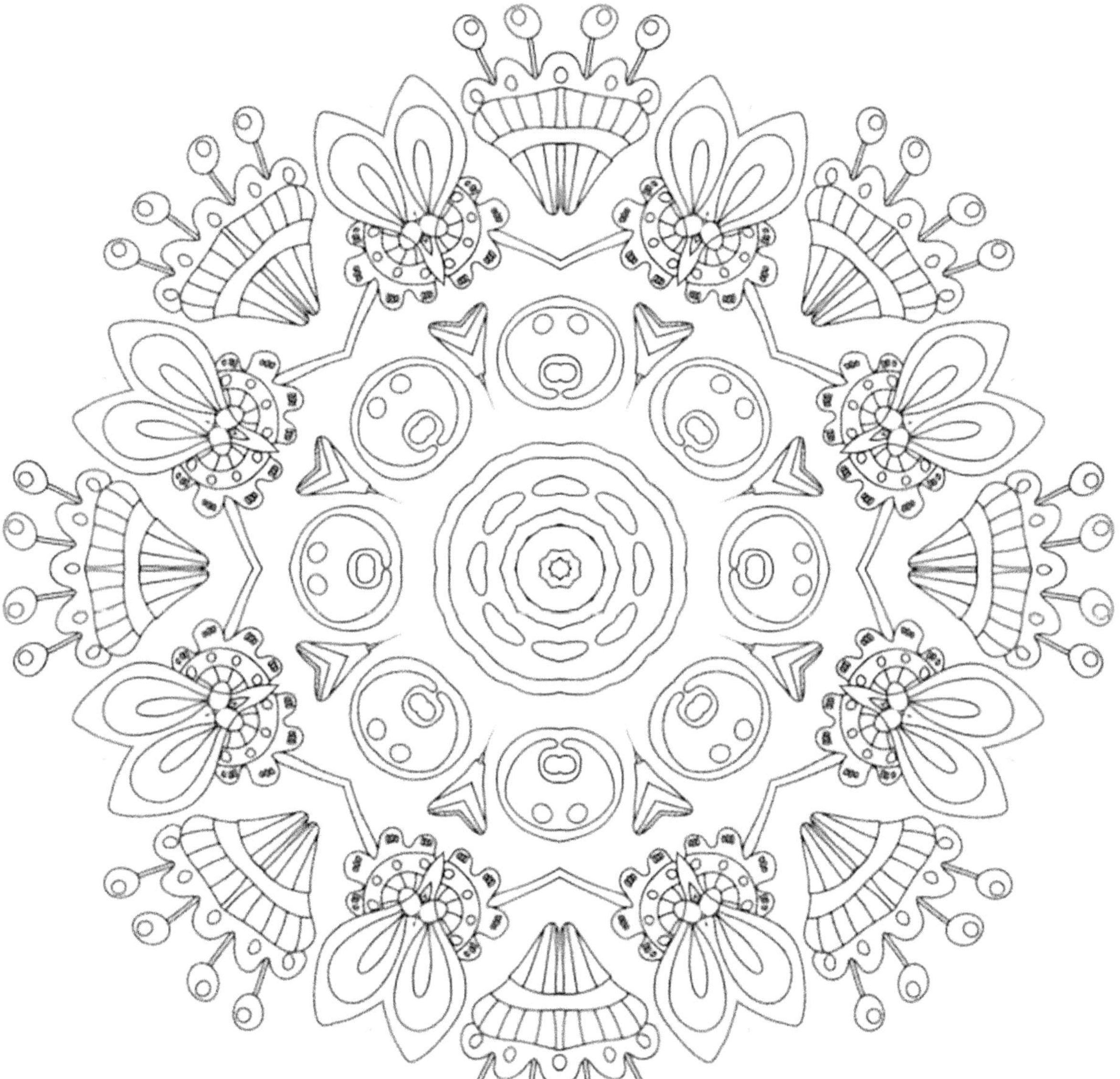

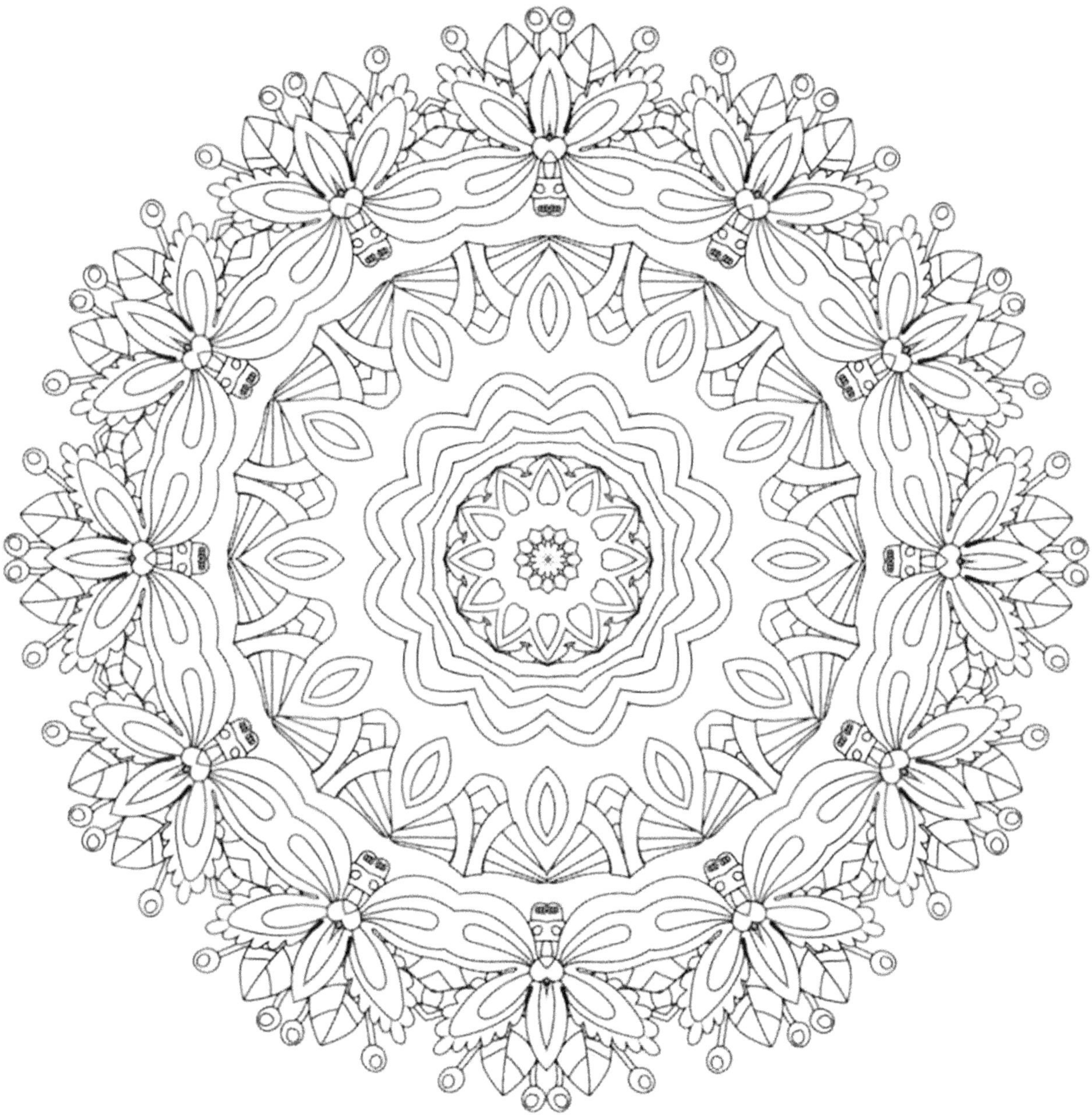

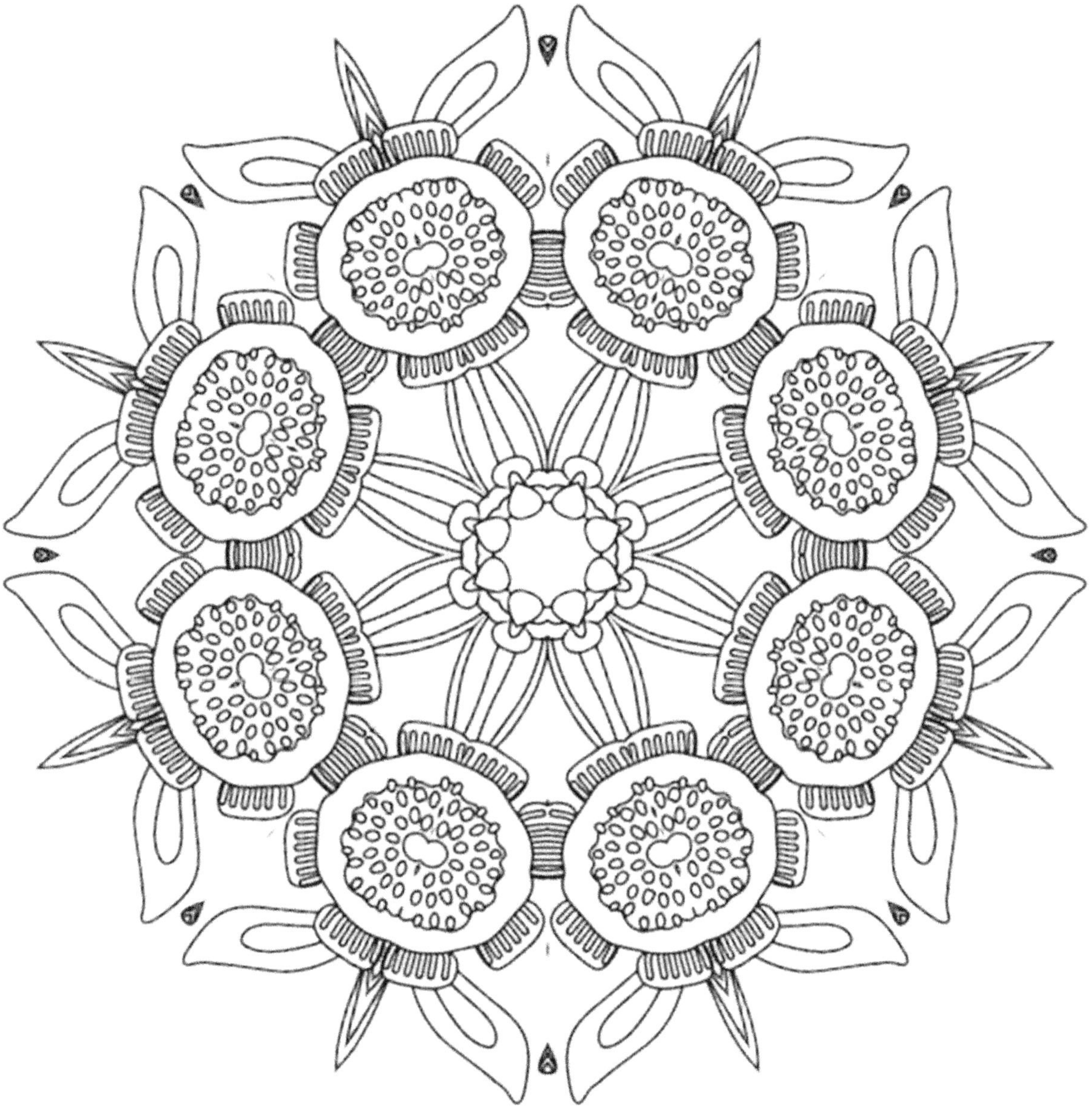

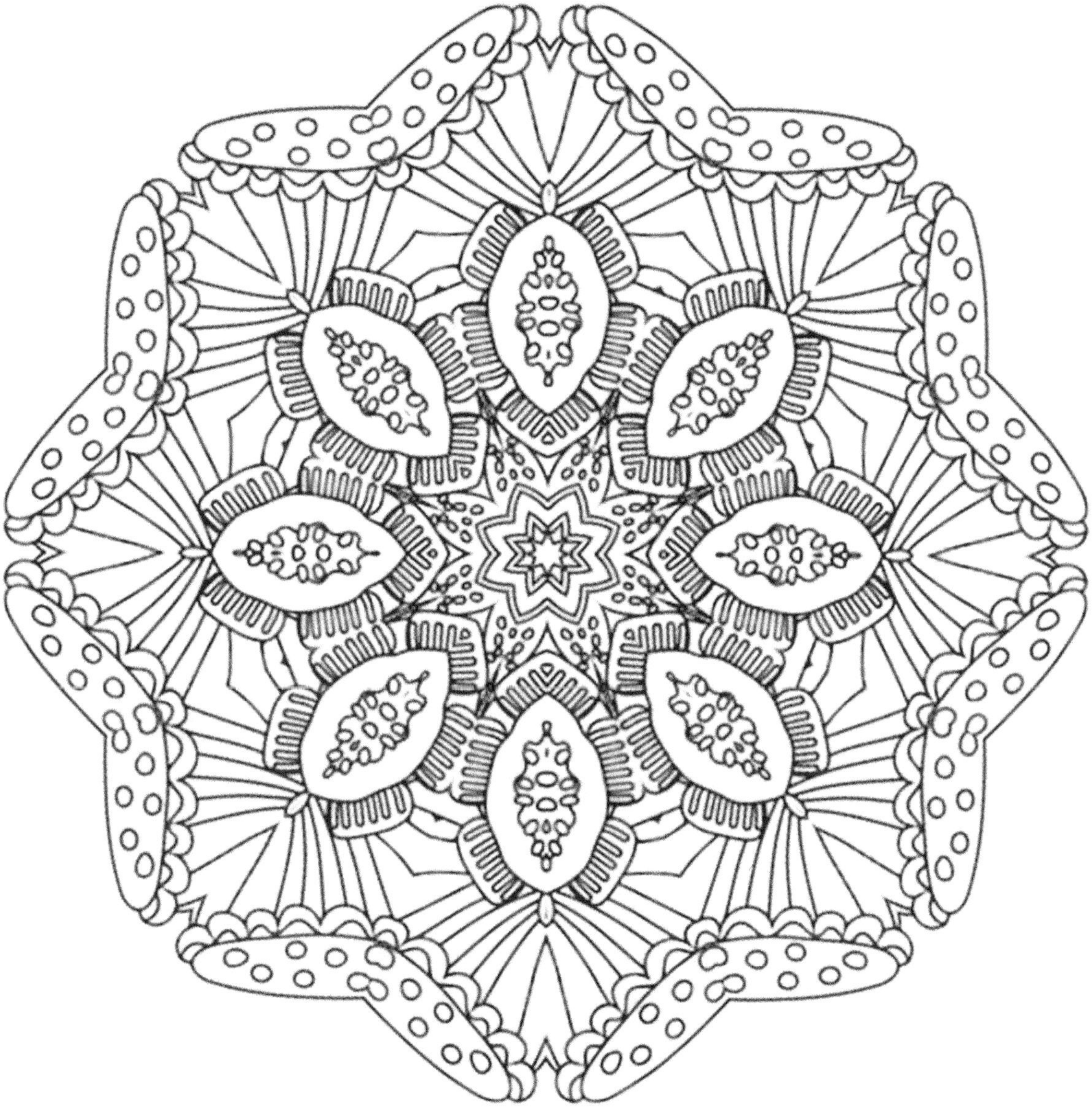

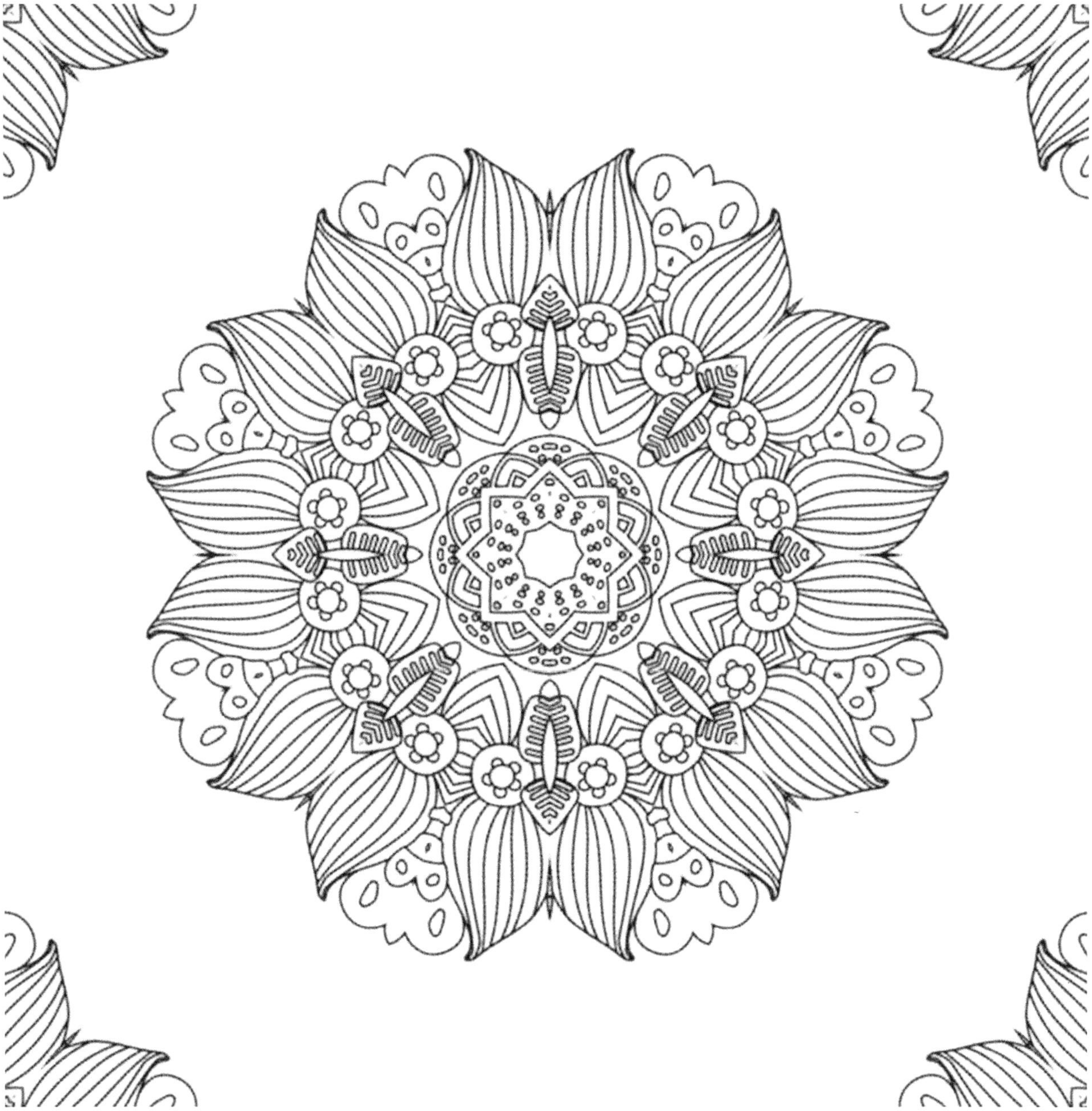

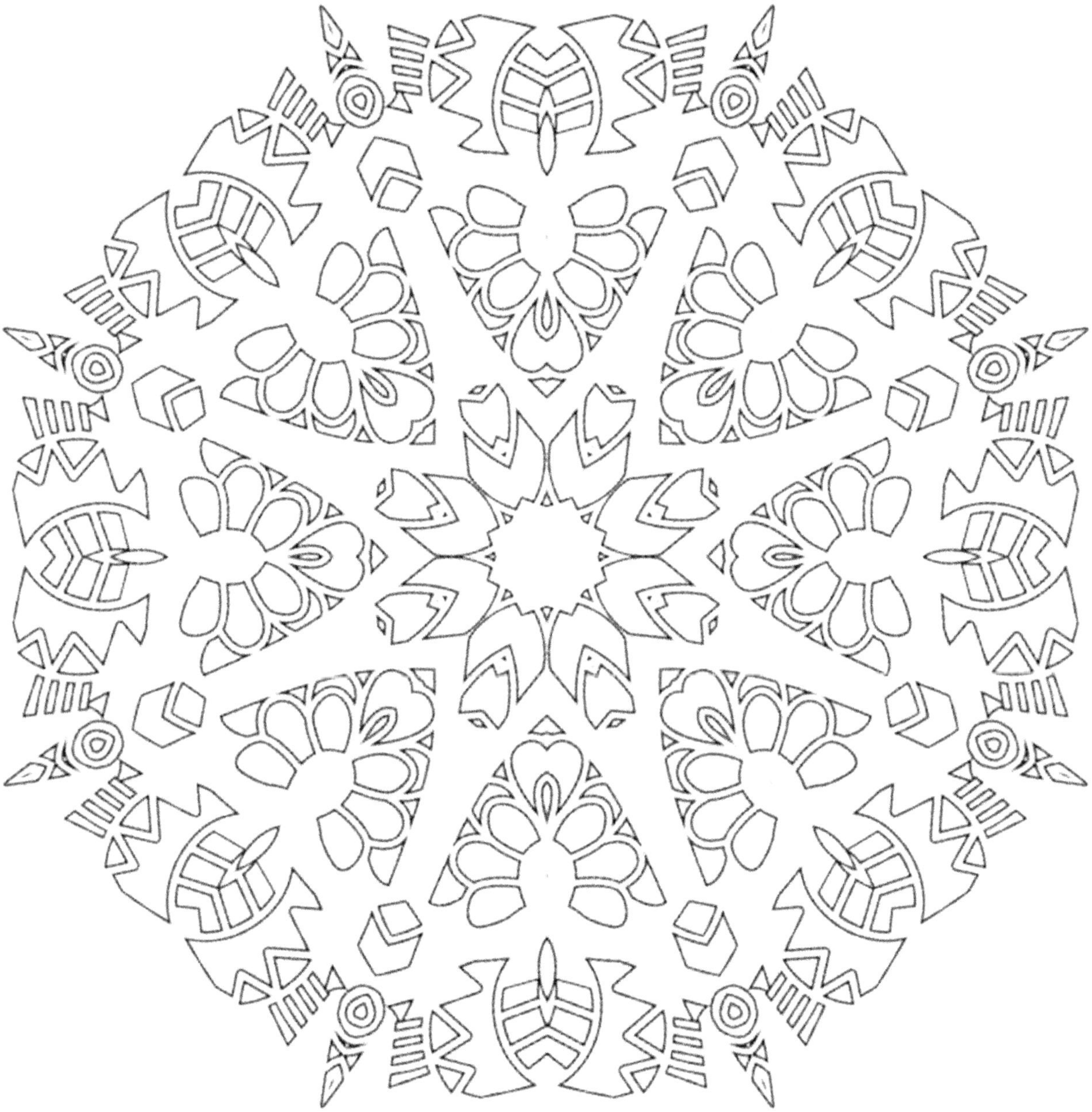

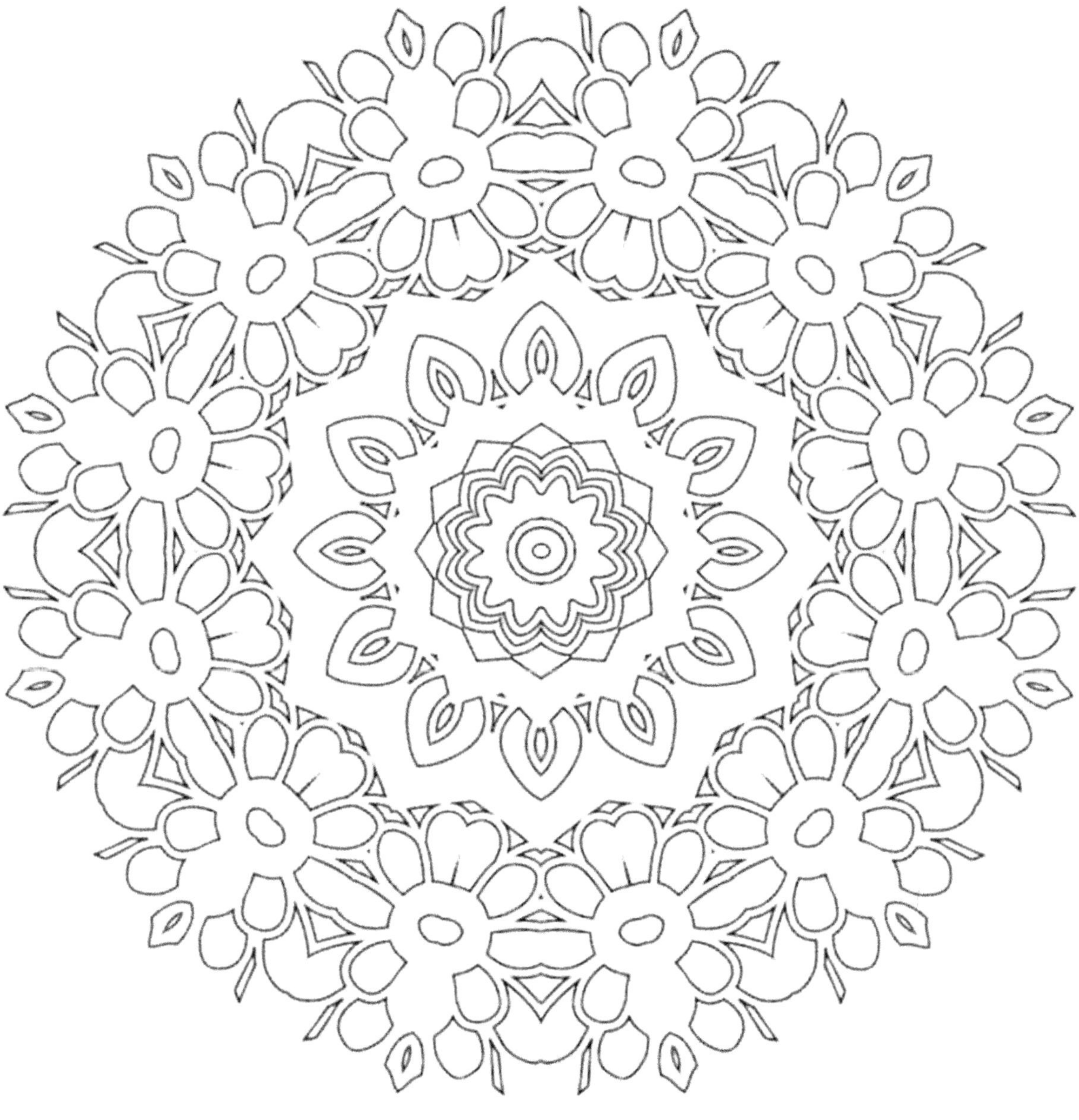

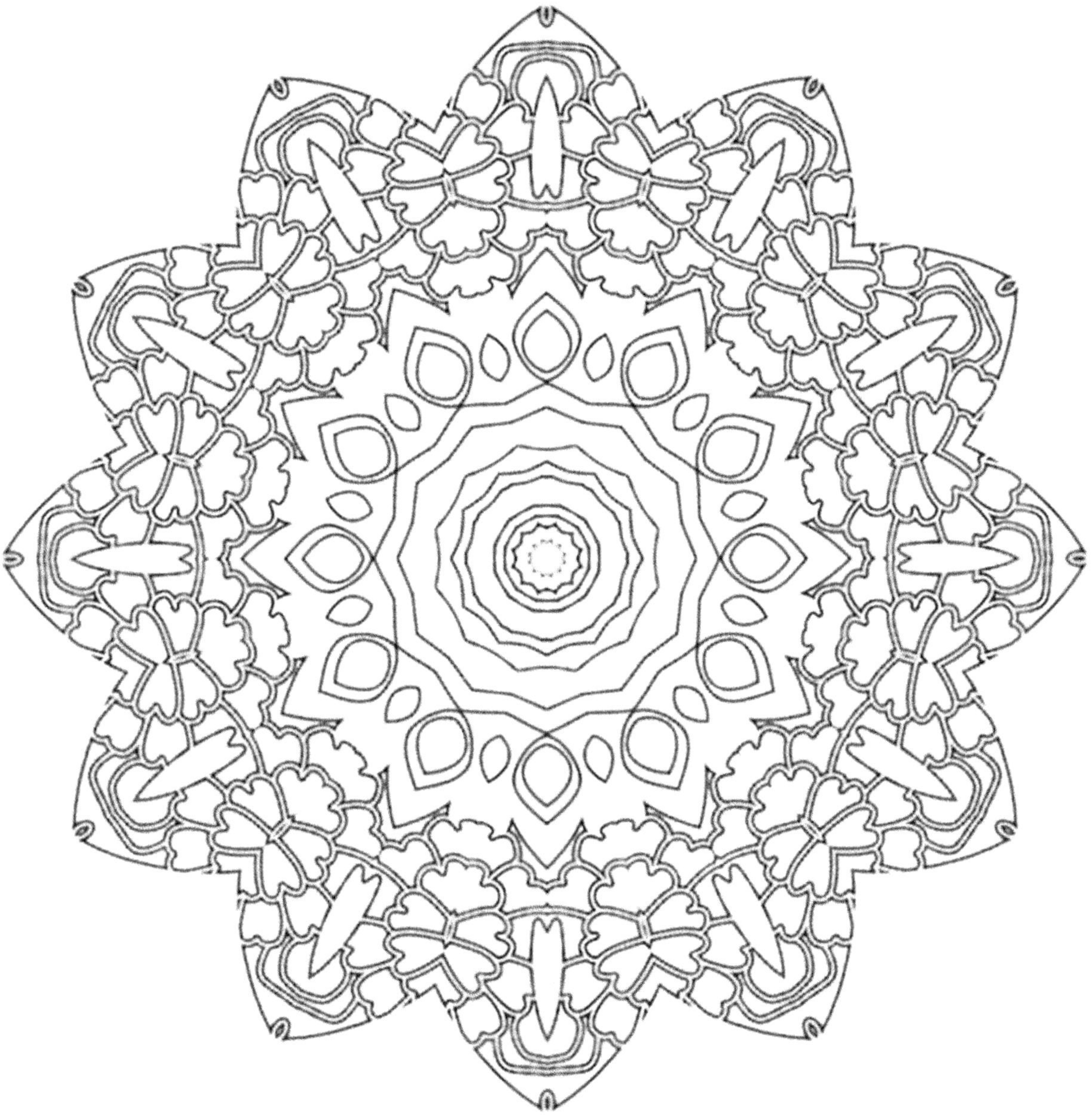

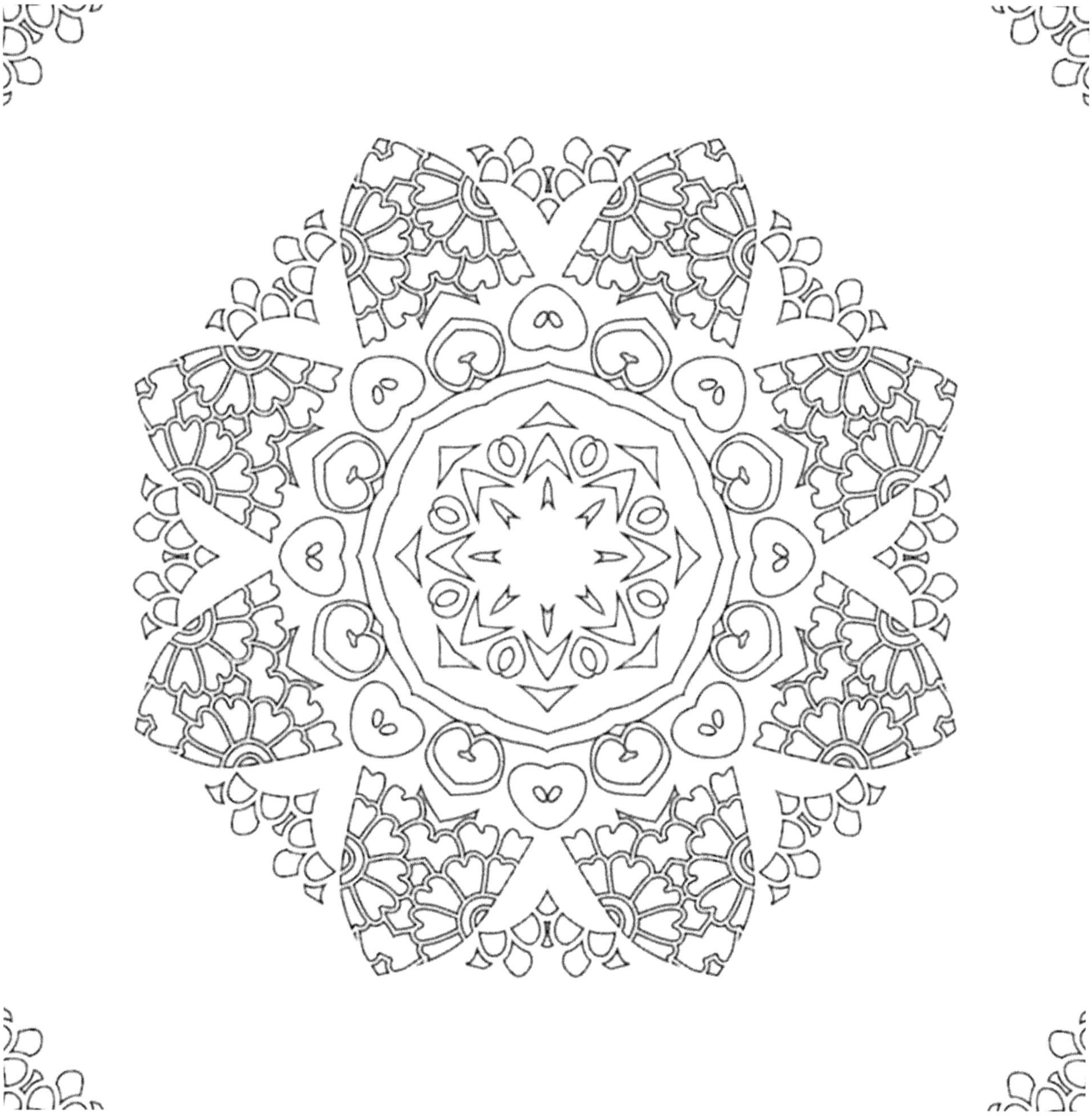

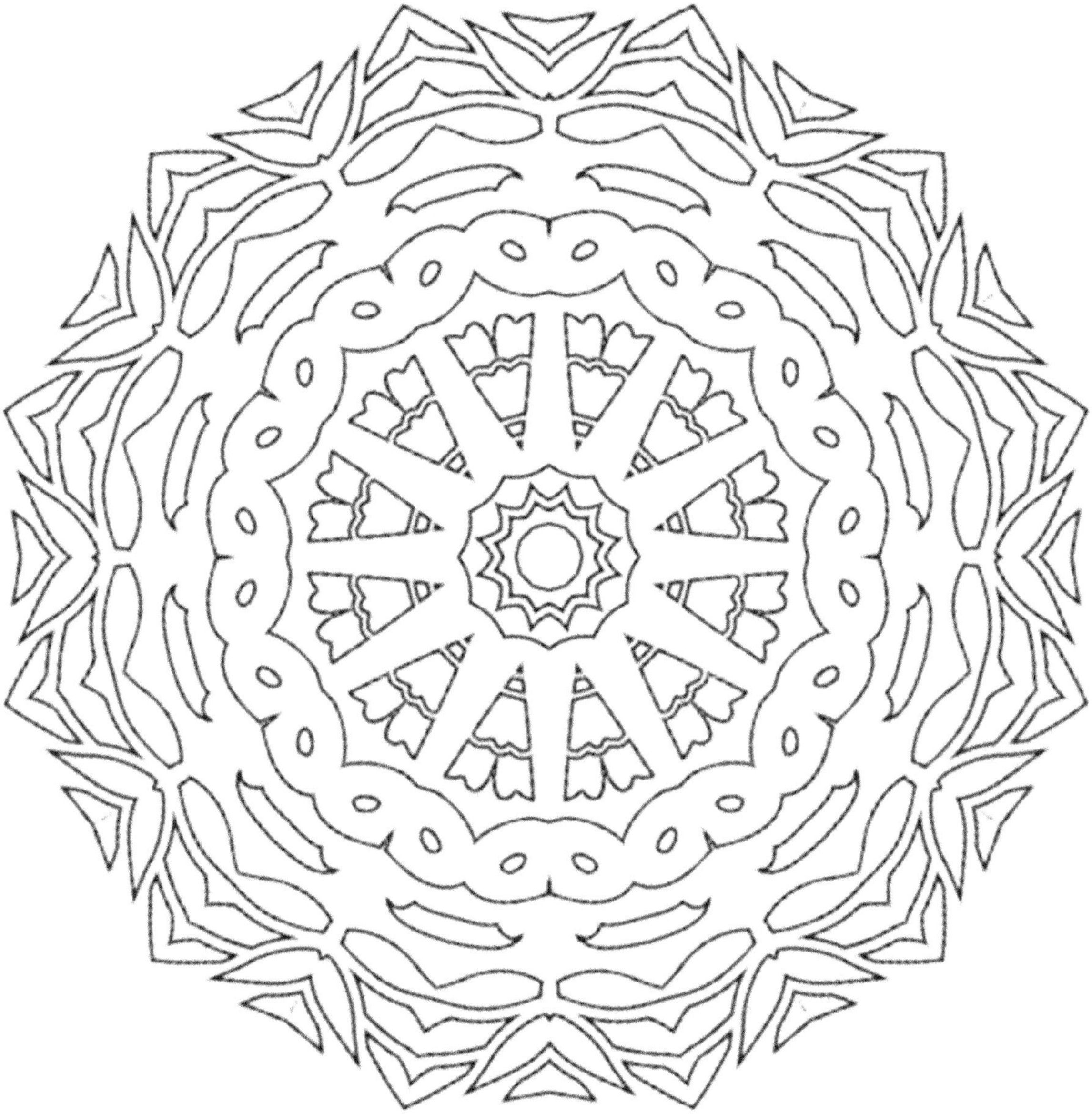

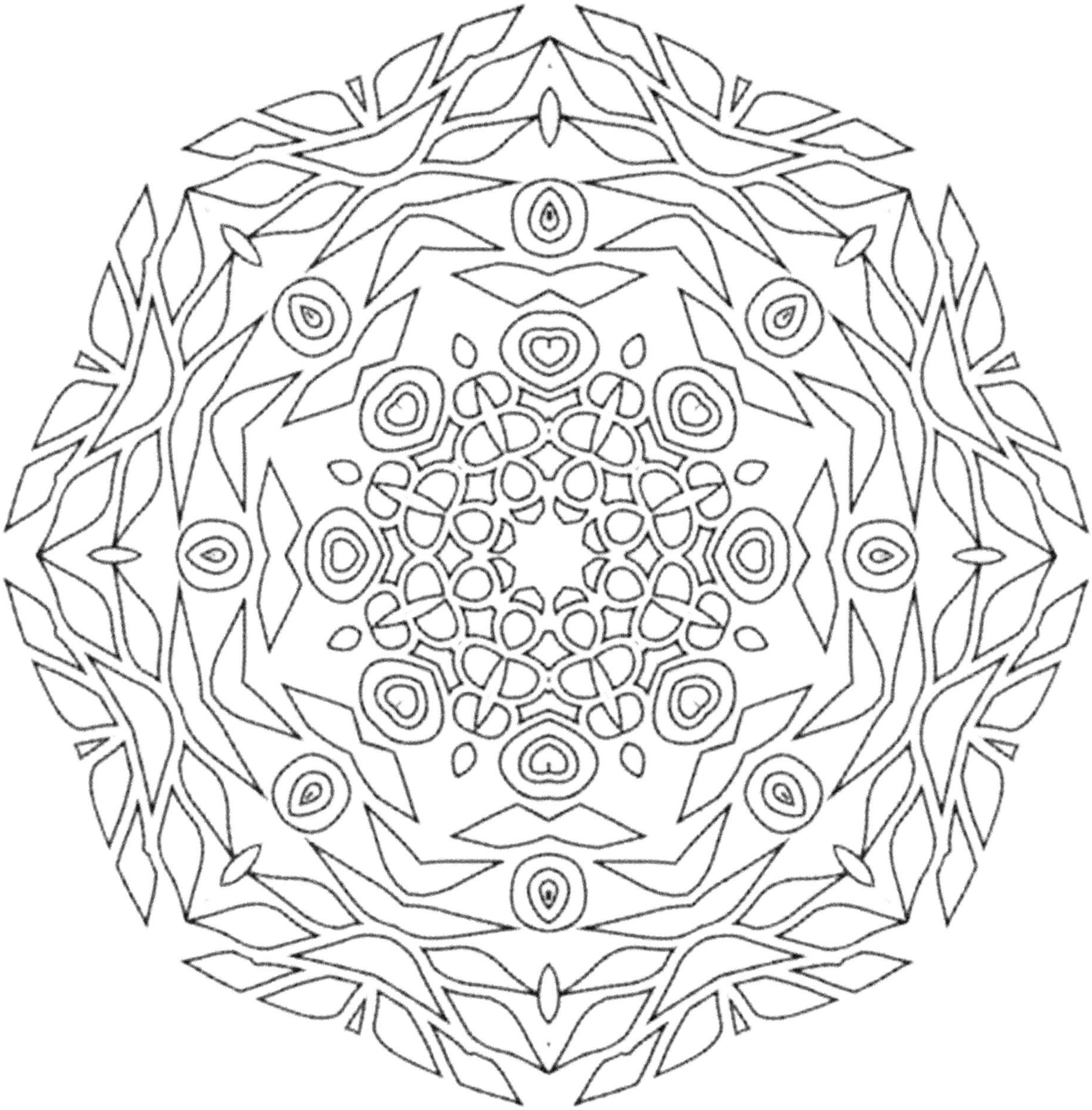

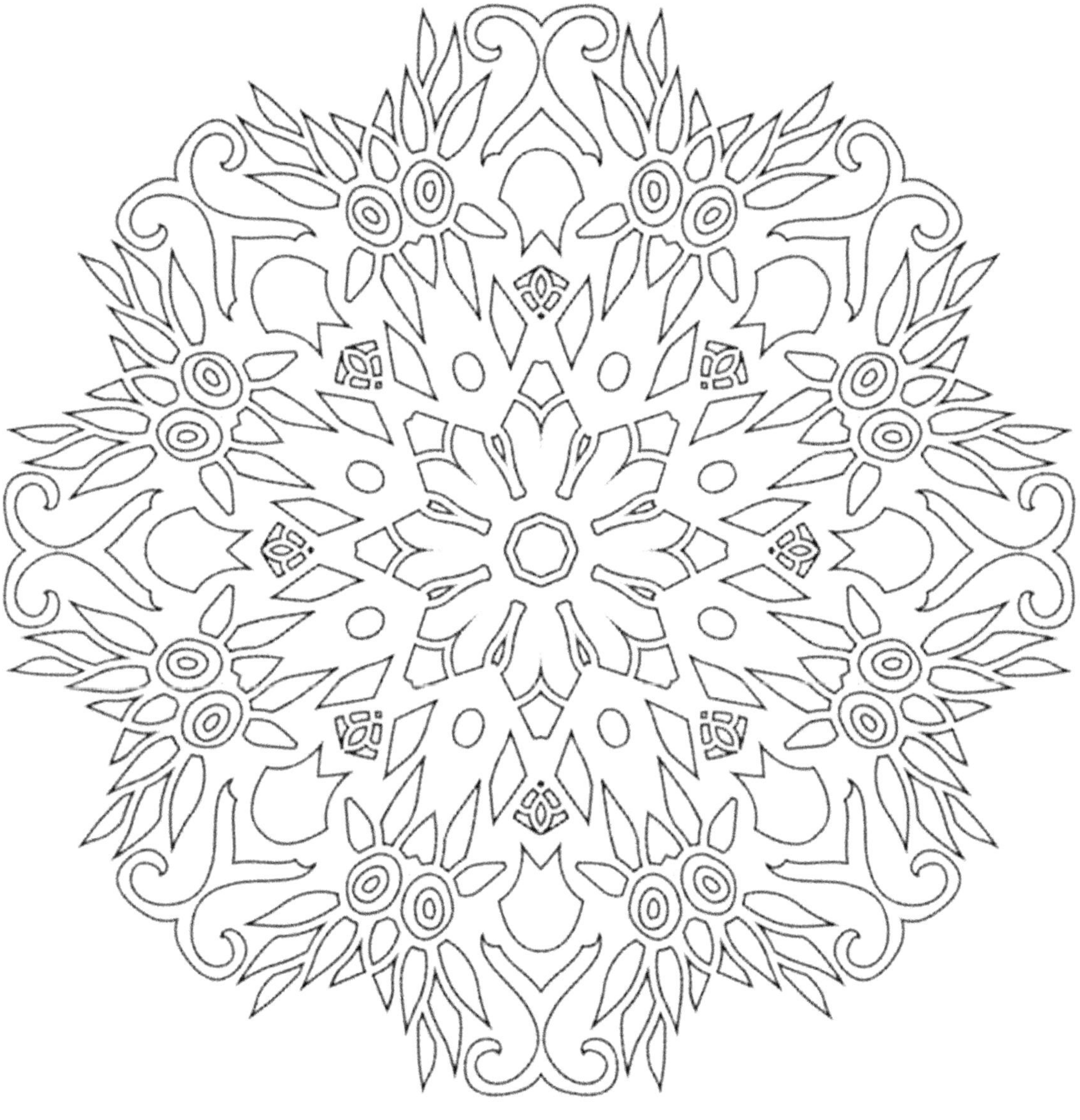

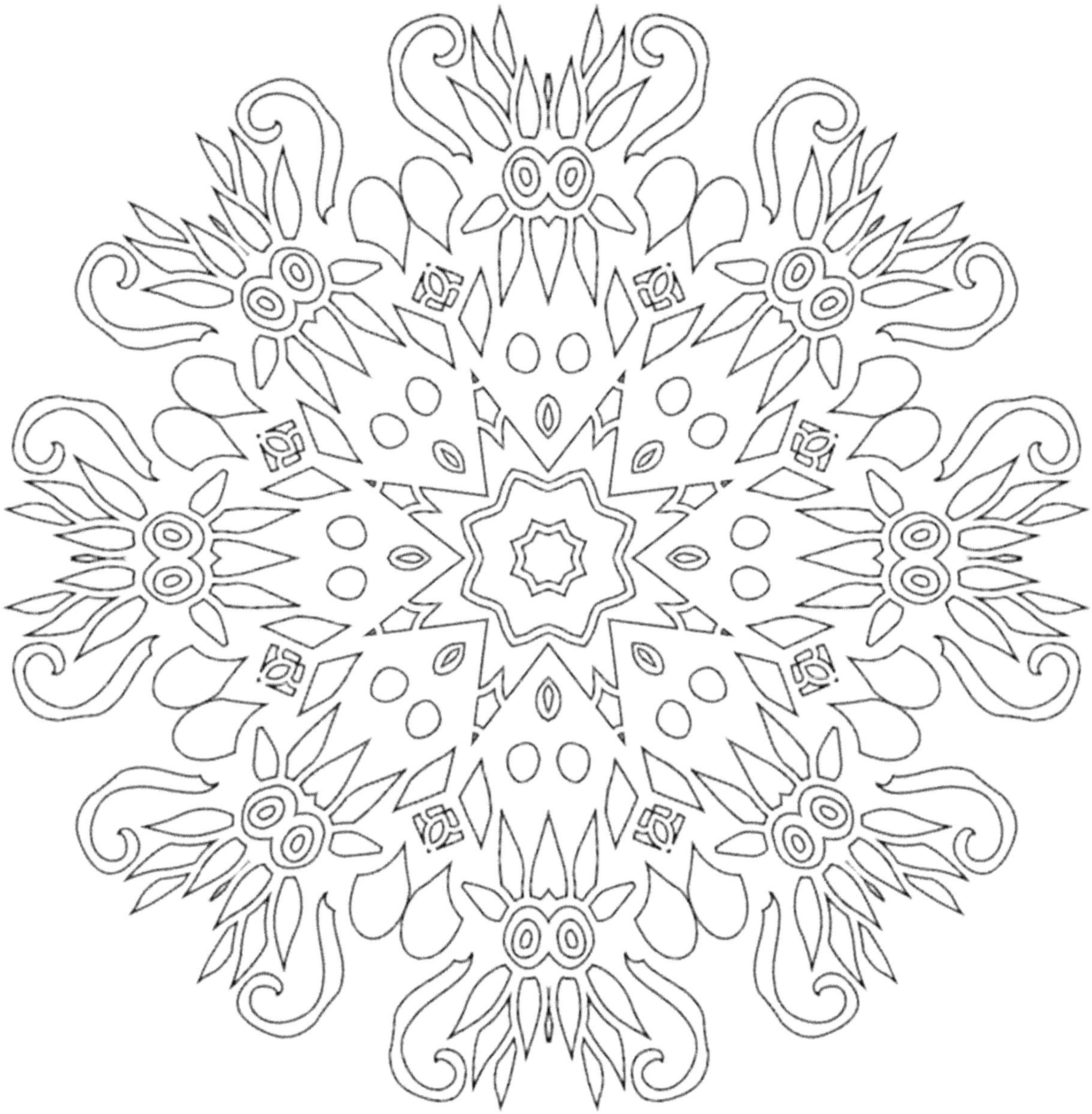

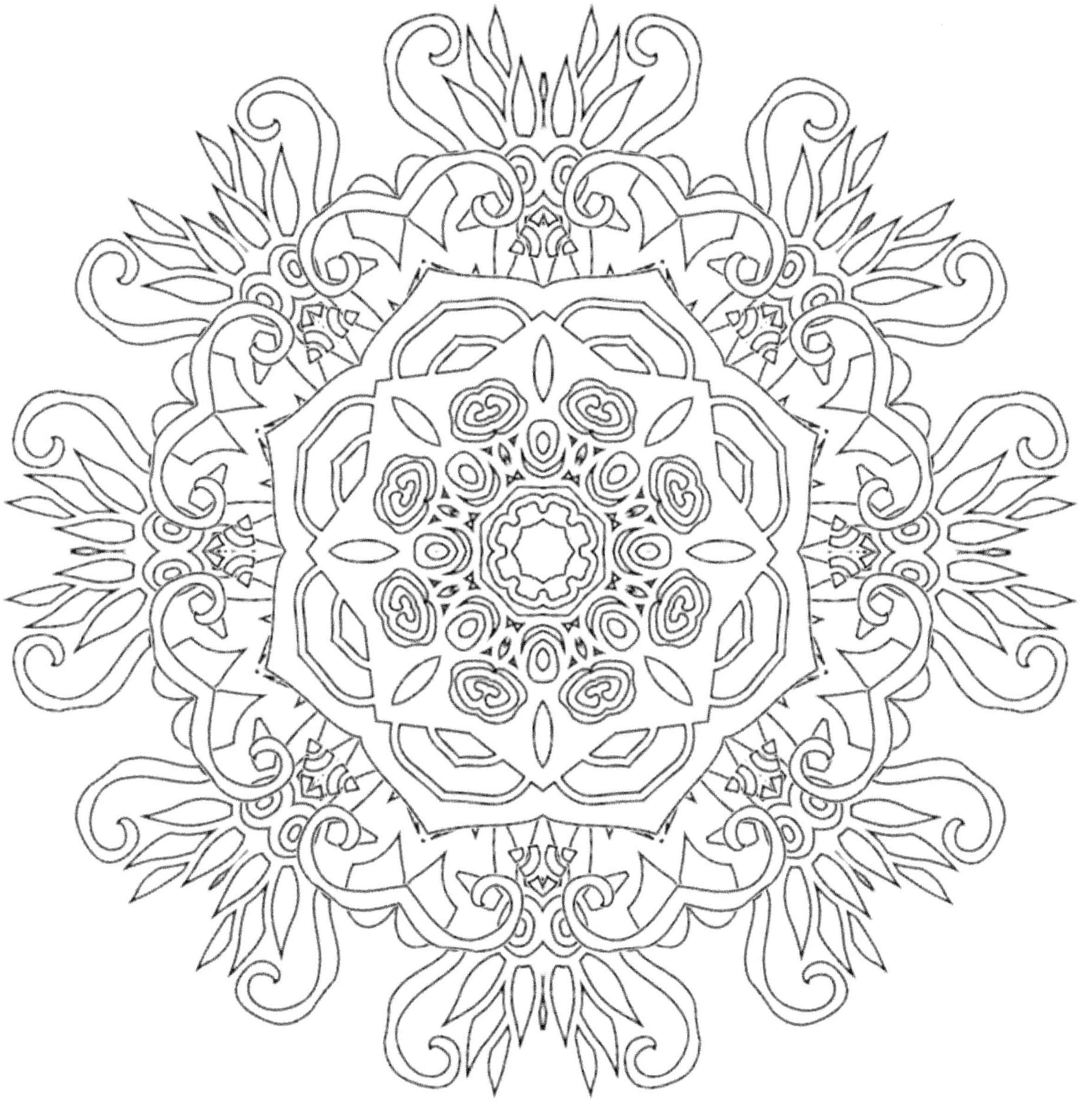

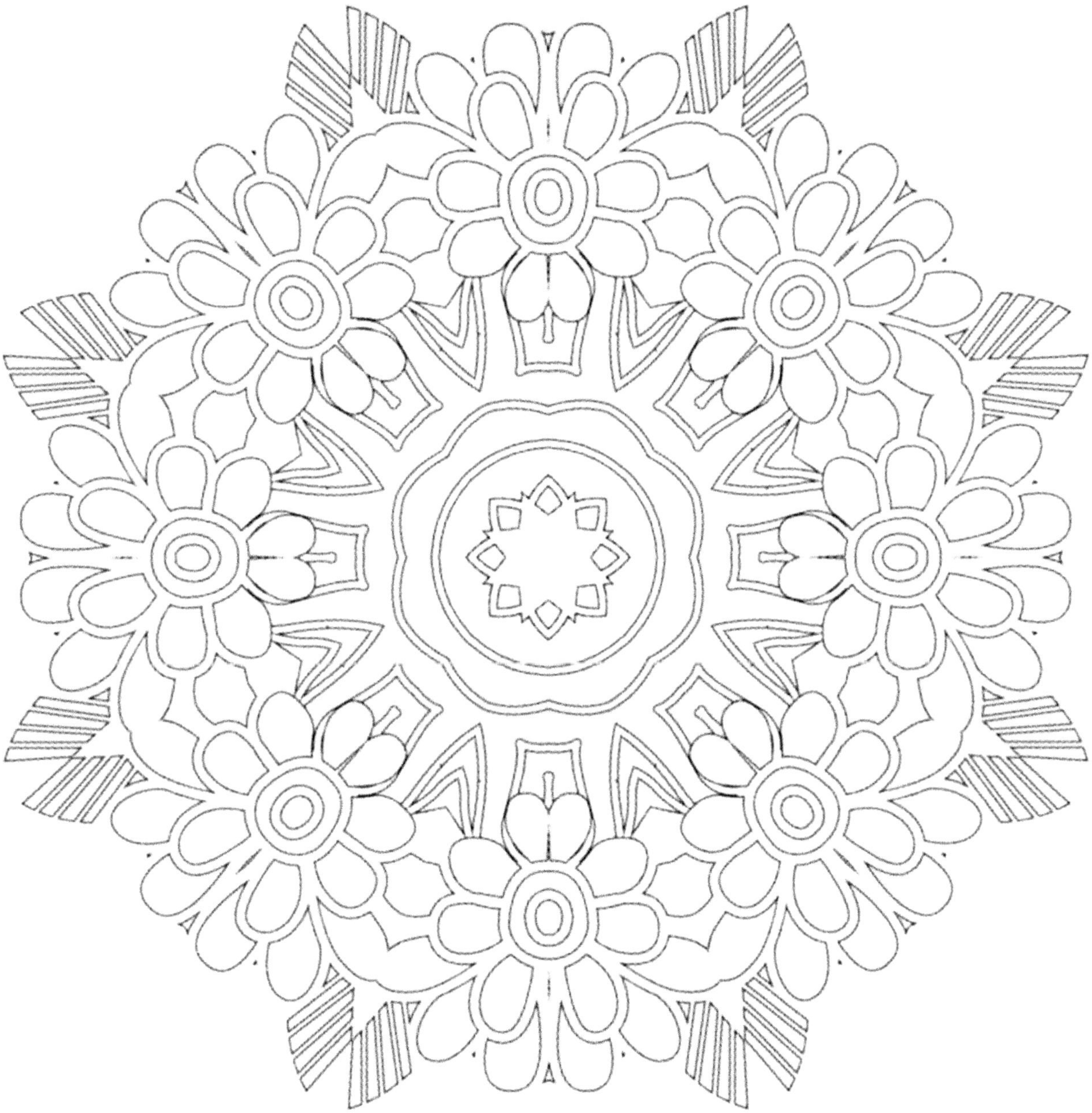

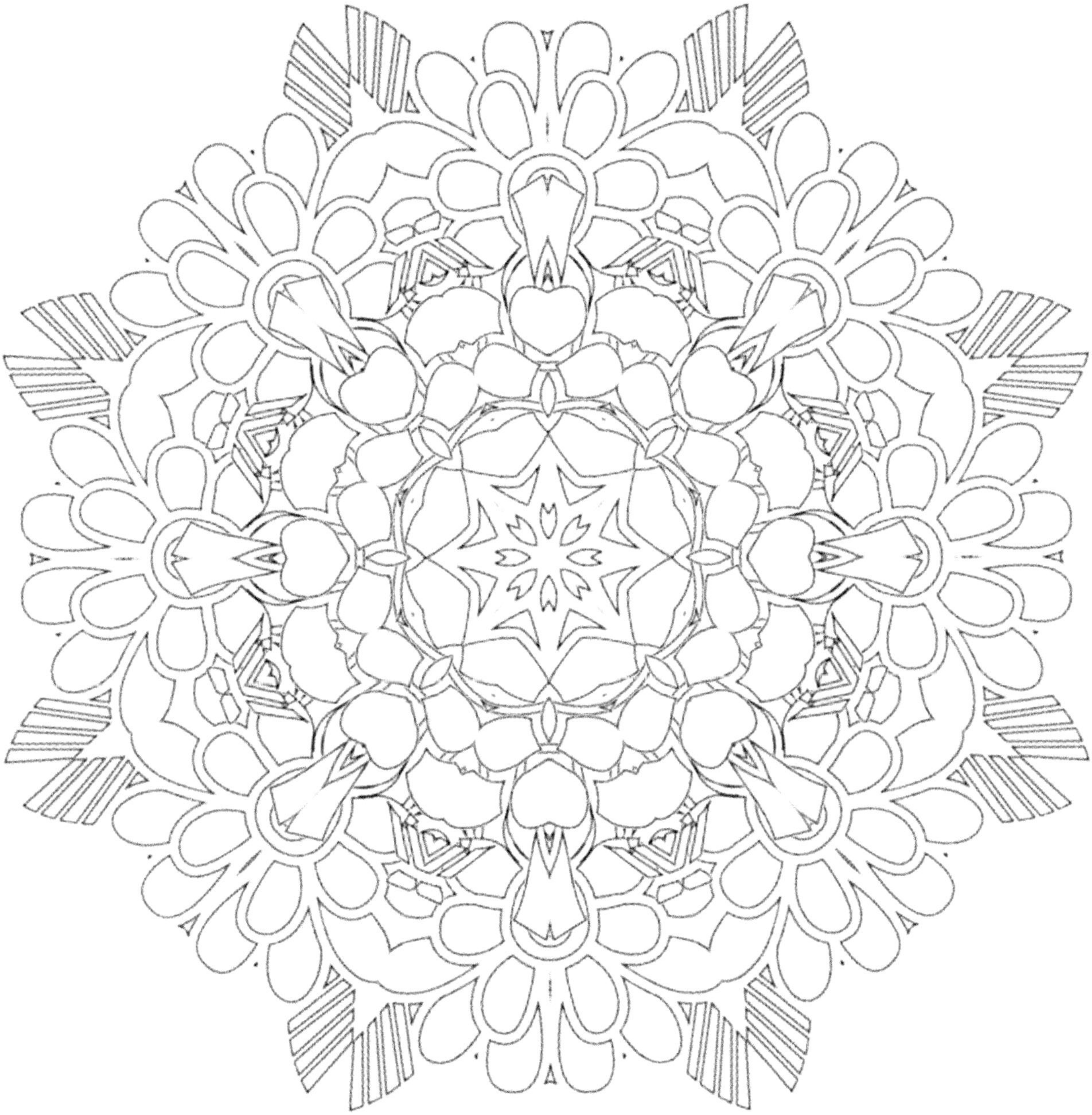

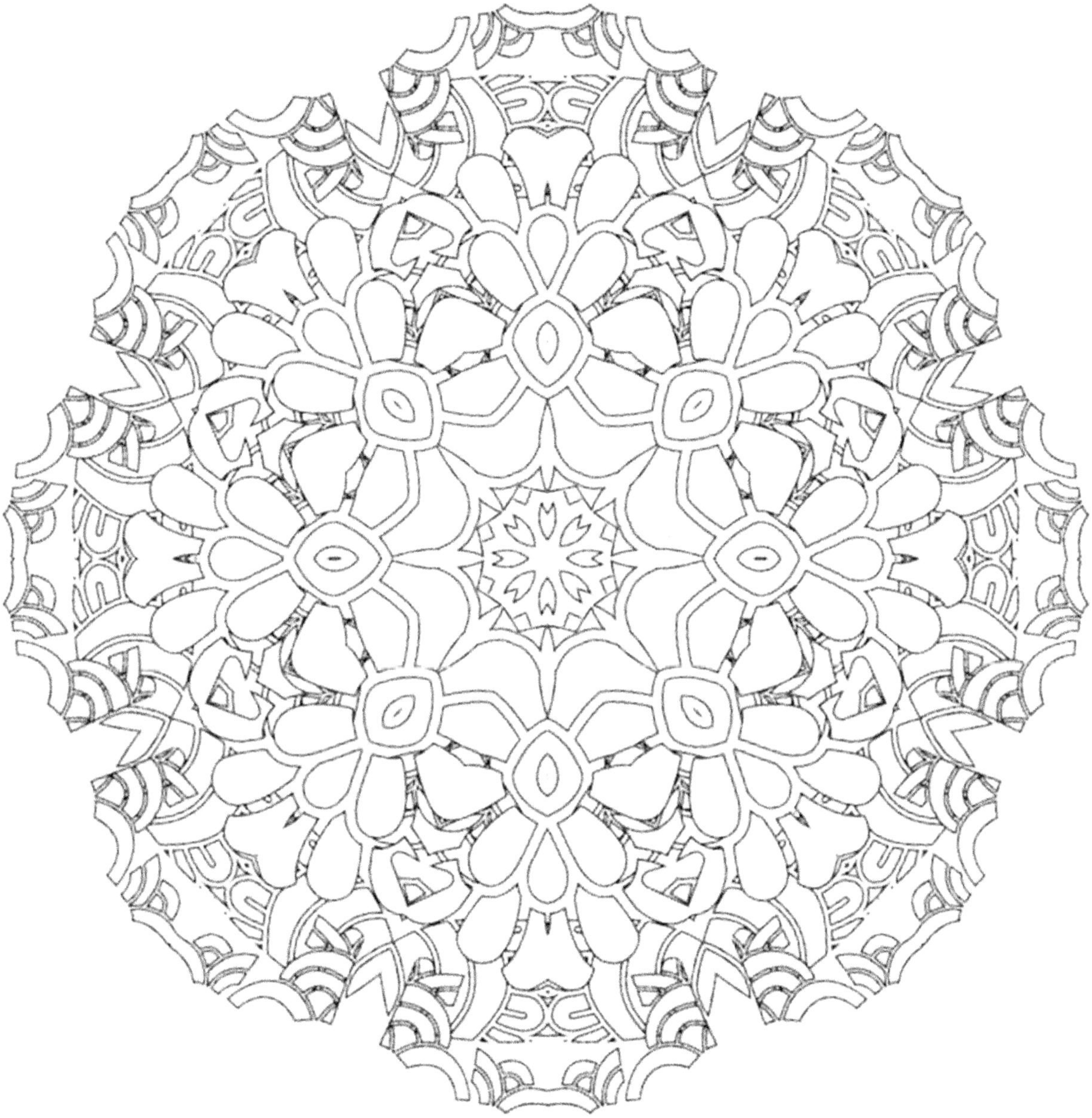

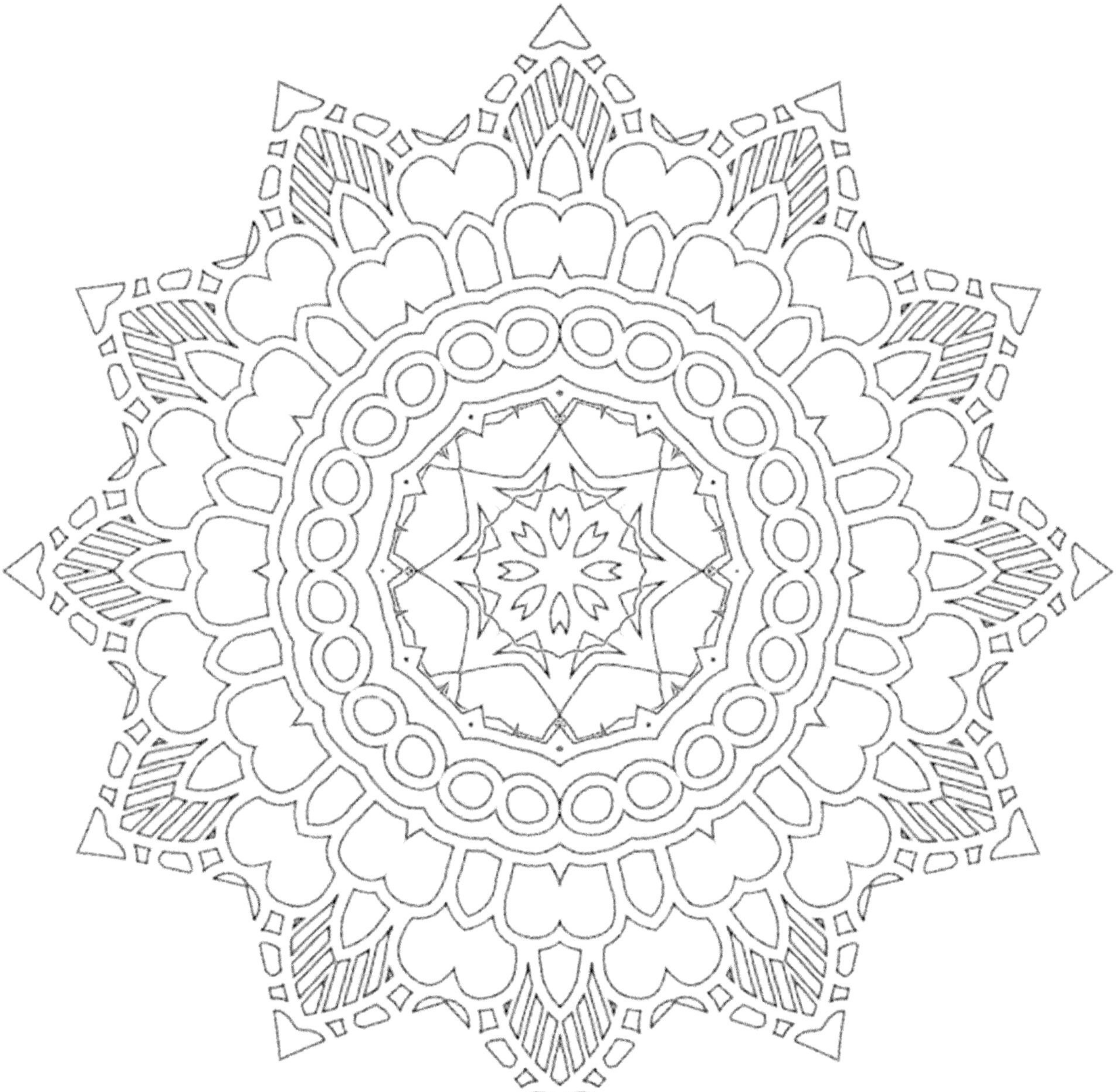

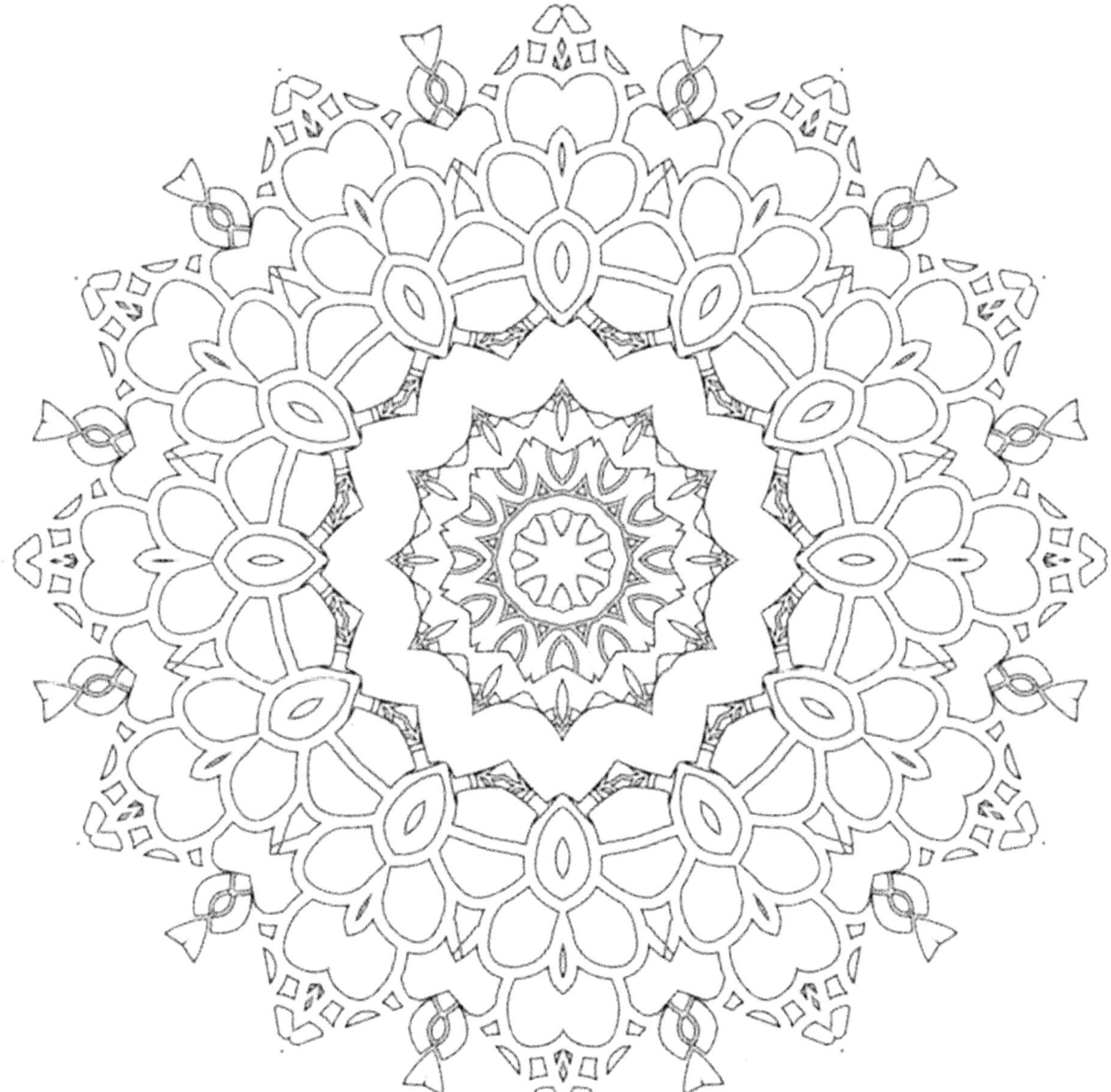

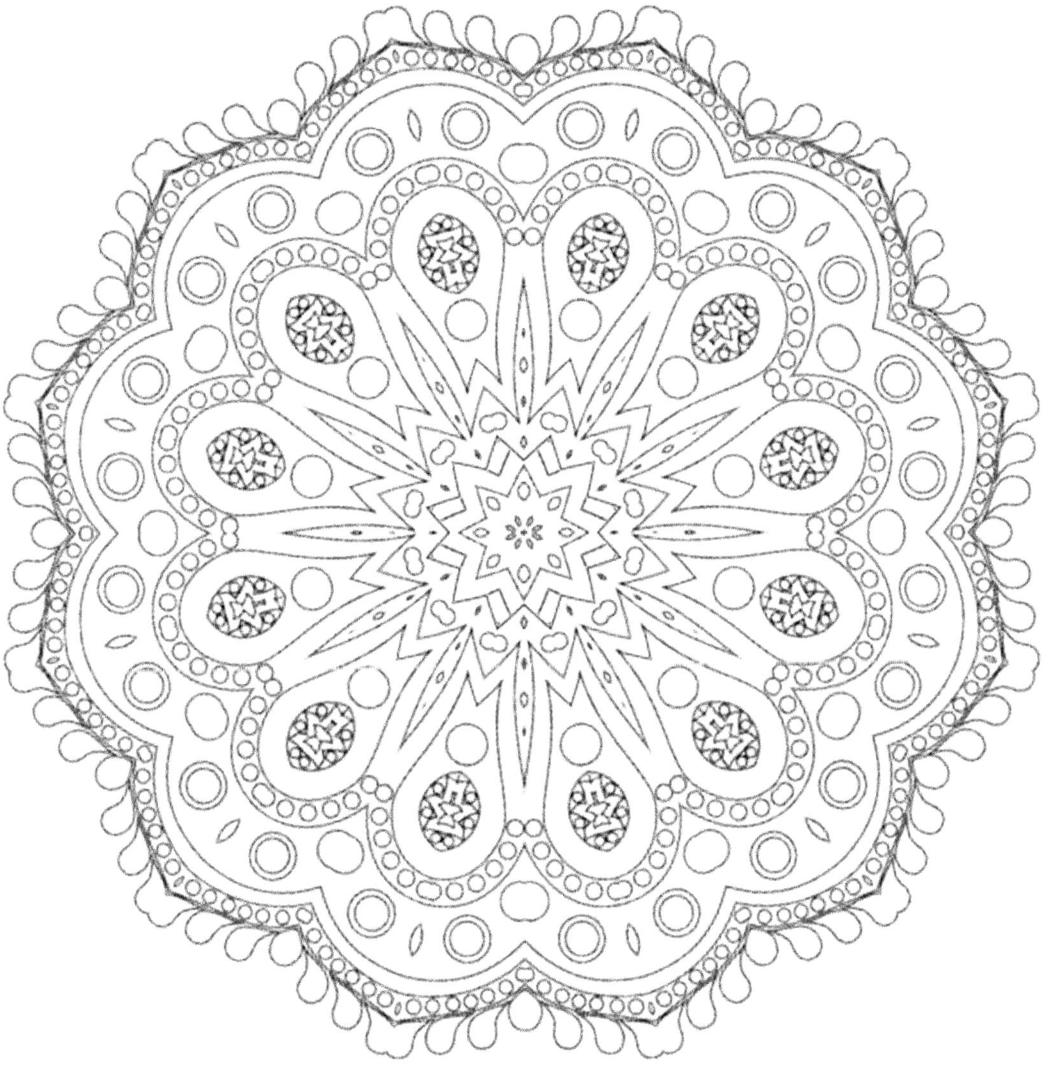

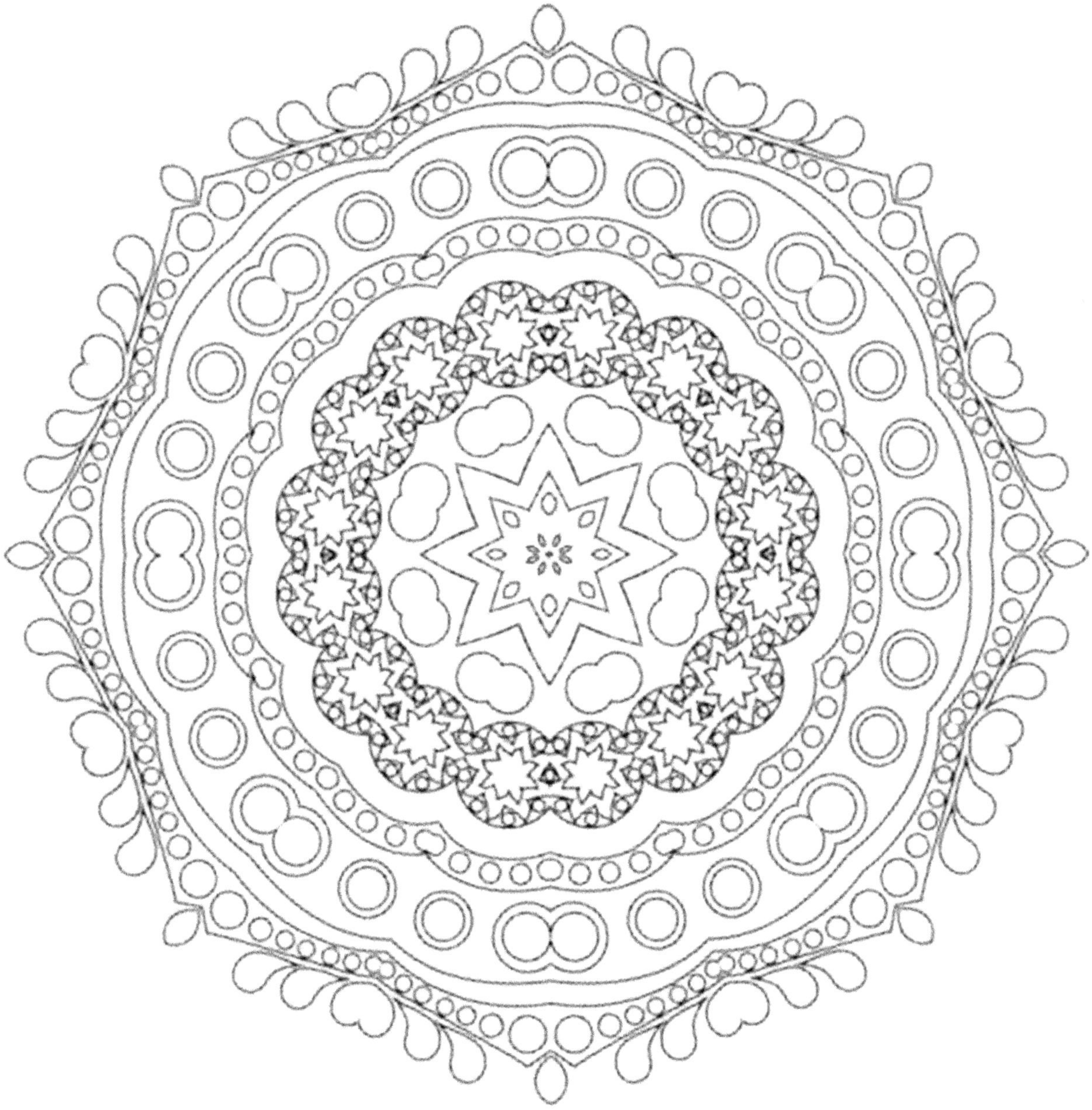

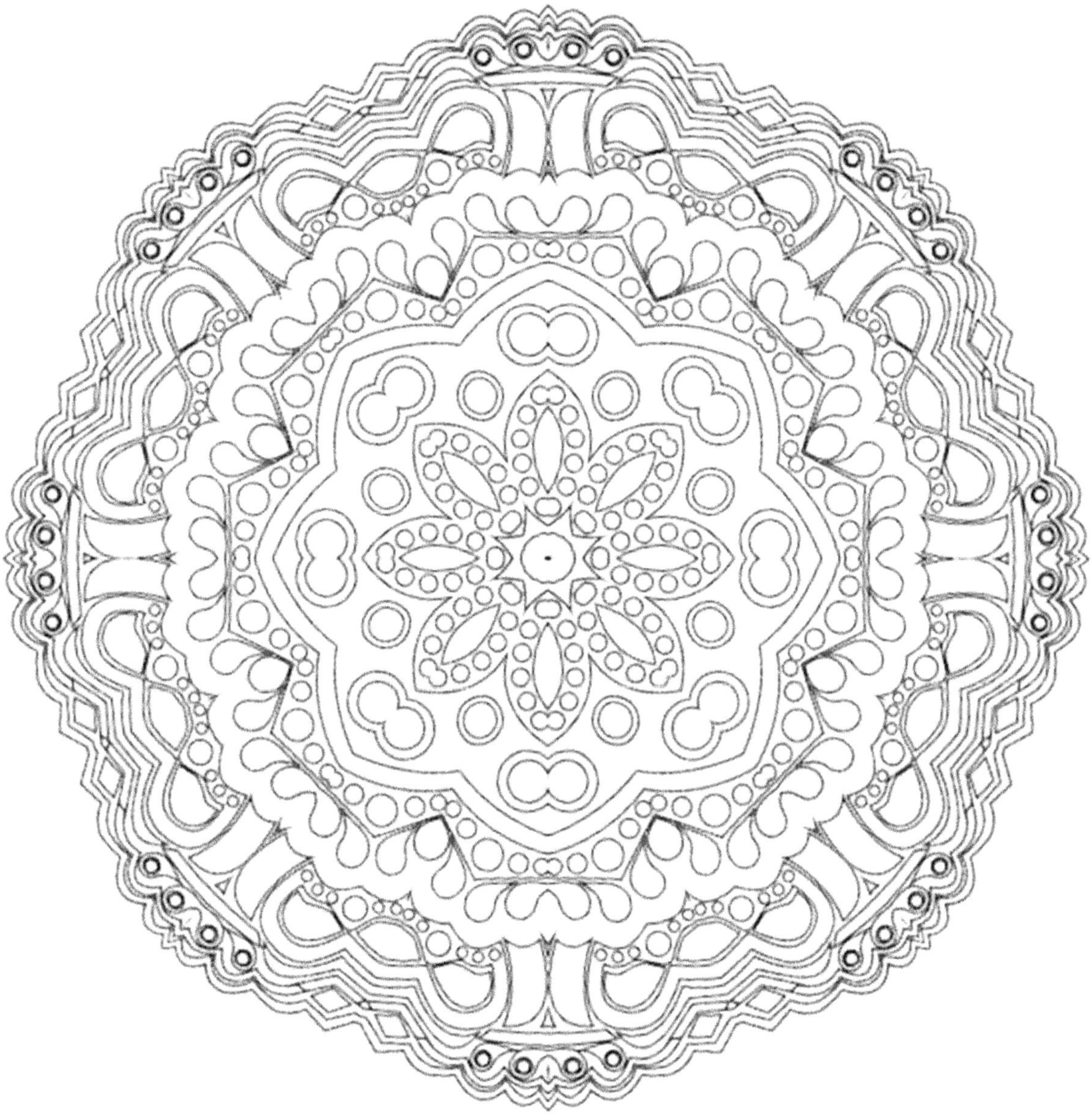

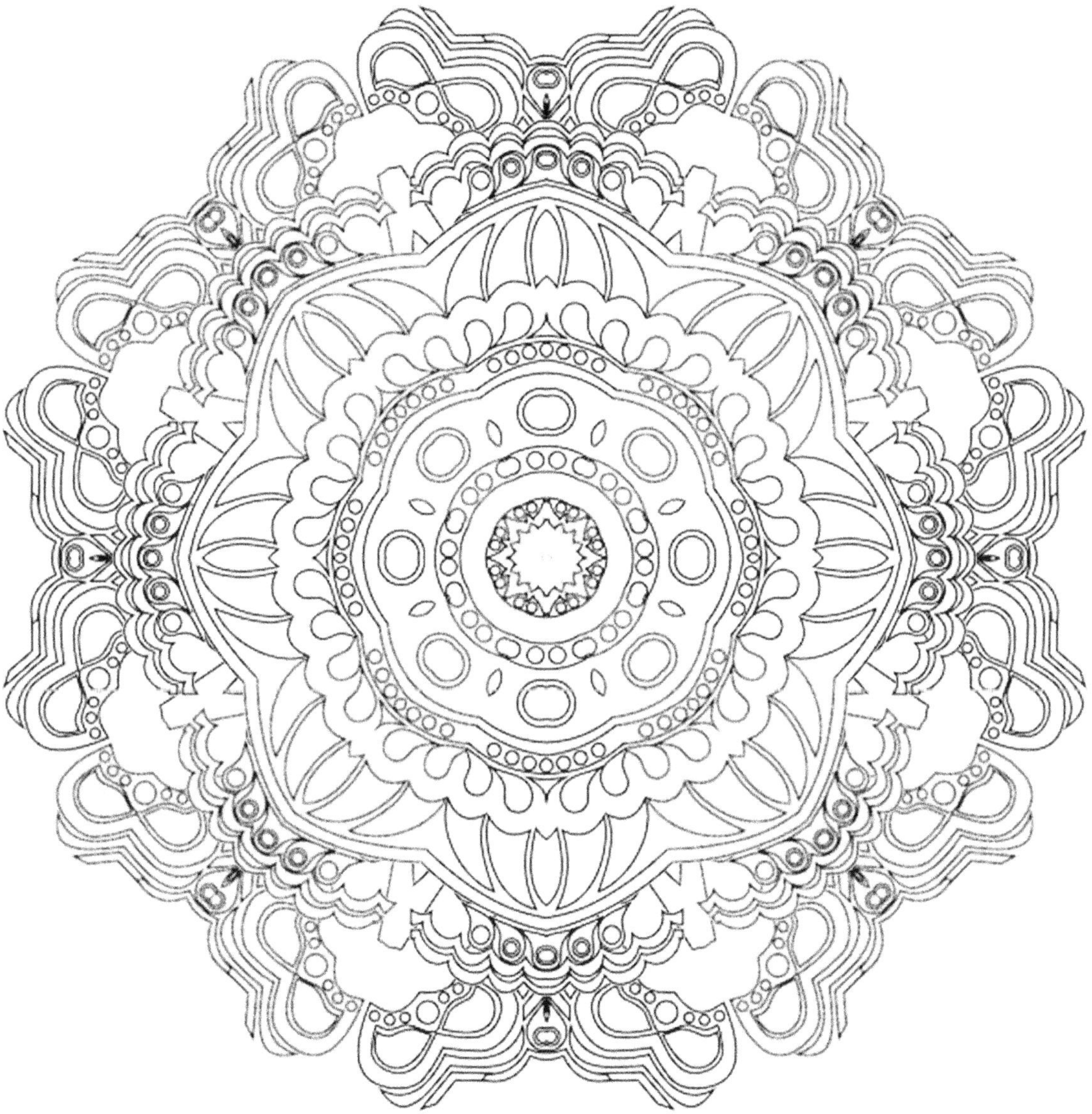

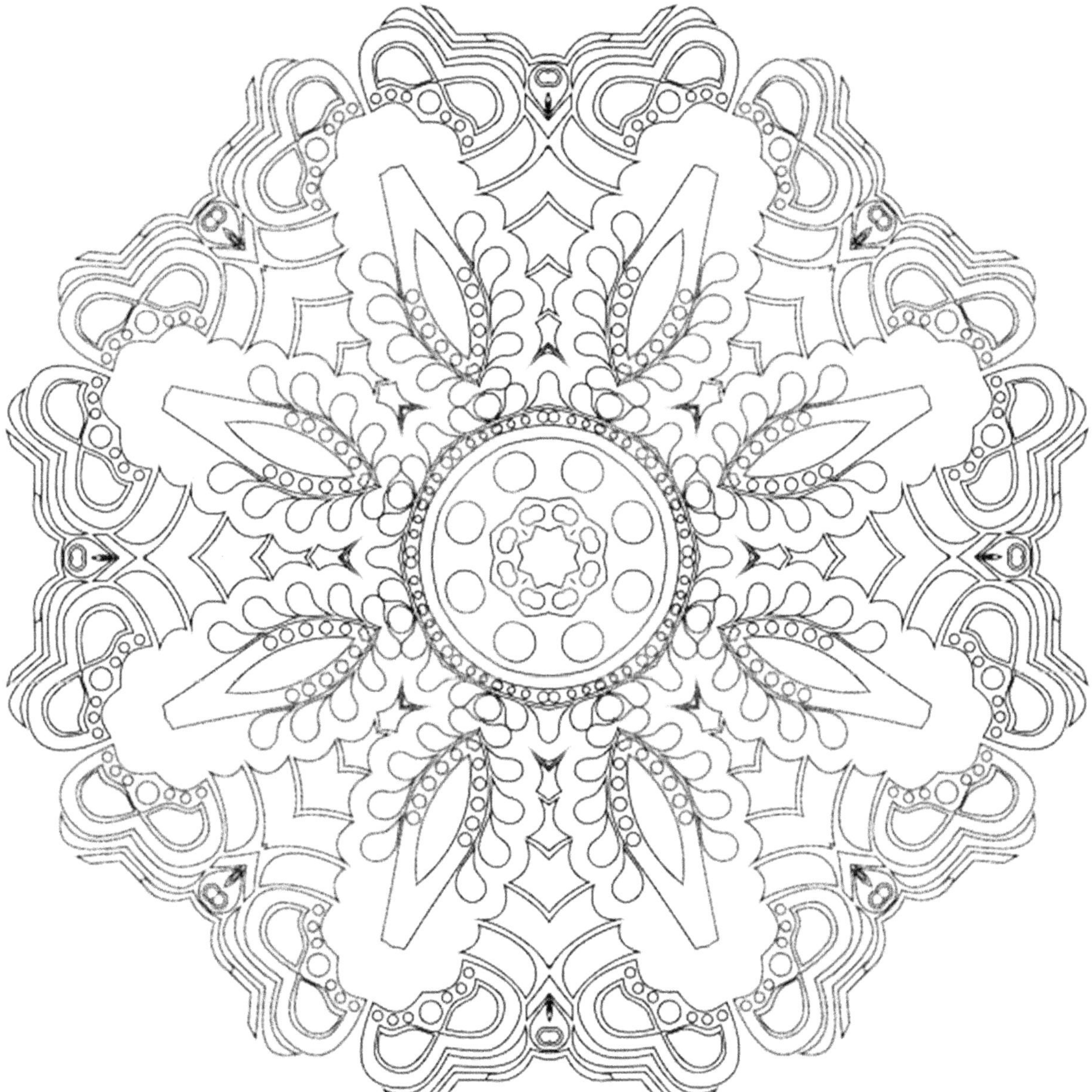

www.ingramcontent.com/pod-product-compliance
Lightning Source LLC
Chambersburg PA
CBHW080553190526
45169CB00007B/2753
* 9 7 8 1 5 3 7 3 5 0 8 2 0 *